# dear artists!

Thanks you for choosing this original version of Ryan Bradley© coloring book. you will be fascinated by the brilliant work in this book created by talented artists.

This book is designed to have differents levels of complexity it includes 50 mandalas with different levels of difficulty. It is suitable for beginners as well as for advanced. it is also a great source for relaxation and stress relieving.

Each image is printed on its own one sided page of thick white paper to minimize scoring and bleed-through.

We hope you have a great experience with this book. and if you have any questions, don't hesitate to get in touch at : babybrad120@gmail.com

Amazing masterpieces are waiting for your creation, Don't forget to share with us your fabulous creations, through the e-mail given above.

Feel free to give us your opinions and your thoughts in our amazon page, it help us bring you sparkling products everytime.

Have fun and let your journey begin

*Ryan Bradelly*

Copyright ©2020 by Ryan Bradley

All rights reserved. No part of this book
may be reproduced or transmitted in any form or by any means,
including but no limited to information storage and retrieval
systems, electronic, mechanical, recording, photocopy, etc. any
ununauthorized reprint or use of this material is prohibited.


The designs in this book are intended for personal, noncommercial
use of the retail purchaser and are under federal copyright laws;
they are not to be reproduced in any form of commercial use.

This Book
Belongs To :

www.ingramcontent.com/pod-product-compliance
Lightning Source LLC
Chambersburg PA
CBHW081235250726
48654CB00012B/1339